What type of swimmer are you?

Tony Lewis

Published by Lewis Parnell Ltd
Copyright ©2014 Lewis Parnell Ltd

email: lewisparnell@btinternet.com
Twitter: @LewisParnellST
Web: lewisparnell.com

ISBN: 978-0-9576982-4-6

Framework of the Book

1. Introduction

2. How to use the book

3. Genetic Application
   a. Definition Genetic Application
   b. Question
   c. Answer interpretation
      i. Natural
      ii. Masterful

4. Physical Application
   a. Definition Physical Application
   b. Question
   c. Answer interpretation
      i. Fast Responder
      ii. Medium Responder
      iii. Slow Responder

5. Physiological Application
   a. Definition Physiological Application
   b. Question
   c. Answer interpretation
      i. Finesse Swimmer
      ii. Speed Swimmer
      iii. Strength Swimmer
      iv. Power Swimmer

6. Psychosocial Application
   a. Definition Psychosocial Application
   b. Question
   c. Answer interpretation
      i. Direct Action Swimmer
      ii. Conscientious Dependable Swimmer
      iii. Happy Radiant Swimmer
      iv. Clear Analytical Swimmer

Chapters 3-6 also include (where appropriate)
1. Overview
2. Key strengths
3. Possible weaknesses & possible blind spots
4. Value to and impact on the squad
5. Communications
6. Suggestions for development
7. Creating your ideal environment – training and competition
8. Motivating and engaging

1. Introduction

The #sportsbehaviour system offers a framework for self-understanding and development. A good understanding of ourselves enables us to develop effective strategies for performance and can help us to better respond to the demands of our swimming career and wider life.

Personality theory can be traced back to the fifth century BC when Hippocrates identified different people exuded different energies. Understanding personality has since been the subject of study for thousands of researchers but here it is applied to swimmers.

The #sportsbehaviour system integrates a combination of mental, physical and functional criteria to the research which has gone before as well as a hefty amount of personal swimming experience.

Your profile is generated from a myriad of permutations created as you make answers to the statements contained in this book. Your profile is unique to you.

I suggest you use this profile pro-actively by identifying the key areas in which you can develop and take action for improvement. Share the important aspects with relatives, friends and particularly your coaching team. Ask for feedback from them on areas which seem particularly relevant for you and develop an action plan so you can grow, develop and balance your training, performance and life in general.

Where coaching teams understand you and your profile, they are better able to communicate, engage and motivate, develop effective training plans, work on weaknesses to provide balance and find things that work and can be replicated for you - all the things they set out to do!

Life is filled with passion, your passion is swimming and you are unique. The swimming world continues to develop and you are a contributor. I hope this book provides you with more of an insight into yourself so you can make the most of the opportunities your biggest asset (that's you) has to offer and you shine in the world.

2. How to use the book

All the categories are detailed in the 'Framework of the Book' printed on page three and laid out in more detail below. Where you fit into these categories provides you with an insight and clues as to how you can maximise your abilities and preferences, what to work on and what to be careful of.

As you go through the book, you will see what type of swimmer you are is based on your responses to the questions. You will be able to see where you fit in within the spectrum and what other types of swimmers are out there.

As we said in our opening statement, your Lewis Parnell swimmer profile offers a framework for self-understanding and development. A good understanding of ourselves enables us to develop effective strategies for performance.

Go through the book taking a chapter at a time. It is important to understand the context given in this chapter so do refer back to it as you progress.

There are four chapters which determine which type of swimmer you are, being:

Chapter 3: Genetic Application. This chapter looks at how you apply your genetic gifts. In applying your genetics, it is likely that you will fall into one of the categories of being 'natural' i.e. easily able to apply your genetics or 'masterful' i.e. will have to work at it.

Chapter 4: Physical Application. This chapter looks at how the body responds to conditions of training and competition. All swimmers will respond in a different way and at different rates. The system splits swimmers into three categories being fast, medium and slow responders.

Chapter 5: Physiological Application. This chapter is concerned with how the body carries out physical functions. Systems in the body play major roles in the reception and transmission of signals that provide your functionality. The Lewis Parnell system uses the categories of finesse, speed, strength and power.

Chapter 6: Psychosocial Application. This chapter relates to development and interaction with the social environment. There is no best way of interacting; but understanding how you do will help you achieve. The system uses the categories of 'direct action' swimmer, 'conscientious dependable' swimmer, 'happy radiant' swimmer and 'clear analytical' swimmer.

Chapters 3-6 start with a more detailed definition of the category and then poses a question for you to answer. The book tells you how to interpret your answer and suggests what category you fall into. You should read the section in the chapter which applies to you.

Once you have determined what category you fall into, the following areas (where appropriate) are explored:

Key strengths. This section identifies the key strengths associated with your type. Your abilities, skills and attributes in other areas are detailed throughout the book but the key strengths section gives you the headlines of the gifts you have.

Possible weaknesses and possible blind spots. There are always two sides to everything. Where there are strengths, there are weaknesses – where there is the conscious, there is the less conscious. The Lewis Parnell system views weaknesses as a combination of overused strengths or the less conscious behaviours known generally as 'blind spots'.

Irrespective of being an overused strength or a less conscious behaviour - this is an opportunity to balance any deficit in the game plan.

Note here that your perception of yourself may be different to the perceptions others have of you. You project who you are onto the outside world through your "persona" and are not always aware of the effect your less conscious behaviours have on others. If you don't recognise any statements, check with others first before ignoring them.

The areas which you could control better or could bring into your more conscious behaviours will be detailed.

Value to and impact on the squad. Each person brings a unique set of gifts, attributes and expectations to the swimming environment and squad. You have the ability to positively influence the squad and there are likely to be times where you have a negative impact. The book provides points you should be aware of.

Communications. Communication is only effective if it is received and understood by the recipient. For each person certain communication strategies are more effective than others.

Coaches use swimming terminology often associated with their own athlete profile and this would more commonly be understood by swimmers of a similar profile. Swimmers are of course able influence coaching communication styles and this section identifies some of your key communication needs.

Read the communication needs of other people in the different categories to help you communicate with the different types. It will also show you what a tough job the coaching team have when trying to get their messages across and that they are not likely to meet everyone's needs in the time they have between sets.

<u>Suggestions for development.</u> Based on your profile, there are a number of things that you may wish to consider to help you develop and improve.

Whether you have the predisposition to apply your gifts in a masterful or natural way, you should review your approach to ensure that all aspects of your game plan are well developed and balanced. You should check that your diet is nutritious and well balanced with proteins to assist you with strength and recovery and carbohydrates to assist training. Fluid intake should be appropriate both before and during sessions. You should take preventative care to minimise injury and illness. You should ensure you do sufficient stretching and blood flow exercises before training and competition.

You should try and balance finesse, speed, strength and power so you have these available to you.

Your training plan should be developed well in advance. You should know what training cycle you are in, what's next and what your target meets are so that you know what is important and where you are going. Competition events should be well thought through.

As a statement of approach, training should largely be built around your physical and physiological type as this is how you will ultimately be competing e.g. if you are a finesse swimmer then the sets should be rhythmic; if you are power swimmer then high tempo sets which concentrate on acceleration. To ensure you are a balanced swimmer though, you will need a certain amount of work in the other styles. You should ensure that your training cycles reflect this. You should accept (if you want to succeed) that work on the type areas which are not your predominant style will not come as naturally to you and often, your returns will be slow.

Creating your ideal environment – training and competition. You are generally most effective when provided with an environment which suits your preferences and style. It can be uncomfortable when your environment doesn't match this. You can use this section to ensure a close match between your ideal environment and your current one and to identify any possible frustrations. The definition of 'ideal' in this system means to suit your physiological needs as well as being the most beneficial to you in development terms.

Although it can often be difficult to change your swimming environment, this section will allow you to think through how you can avoid or influence areas of possible frustrations or where things are a long way from your ideal. This is an important section for you to share with the coaching team.

For your happiness, training should largely be built around your physical and physiological type as this will be the most comfortable for you and give you a sense of achievement. The ideal (in the sense of most beneficial) environment will however be one where the workload is split across the types so that it is both interesting and you are developing the full range of attributes.

Motivating and engaging. It is said that it is not possible to motivate everyone - only to provide the environment in which they will motivate themselves. Here are some suggestions which can help to provide you with motivation and ensure you are engaged. Try and create the environment which best suits you and share this with your coaching team.

For you to be motivated and engaged there should be something in training which is in direct response to your physical and physiological type. This will allow you to practice your race craft and just be magnificent at what you do best.

Your current environment should be as closely aligned to your ideal environment as possible. Making small changes in this area will help you to be motivated and engaged. Part of this will be effective communications, in the style which suits you best.

Competition events should also reflect your physical and physiological type. On the spectrum this would mean generally that finesse and speed swimmers would benefit from a wider range and possibly longer events to develop their efficiency and rhythm as well as engage in longer battles with competitors; whilst power and strength swimmers generally prefer shorter distance with tussles and blasts.

Whilst you should concentrate on your own category on the first reading, you should also have mind to look at the other categories as this will help you understand what types your team mates and competitors are, their strengths and weaknesses and how you would best communicate with them.

3. Genetic Application

People are sometimes referred to as 'gifted' and 'talented' and these terms are usually applied to a small percentage of the population. In truth, we all have genetic gifts and you'll have these in varying amounts.

The system identifies, in board terms, how you apply your genetic gifts. In applying your genetics, it is likely that you will fall into one of the categories of being 'natural' i.e. easily able to apply your genetics or 'masterful' i.e. will have to work at it.

It may appear on the face of it that 'natural' swimmers are advantaged and will be the ones to achieve. It is important to state that 'masterful' swimmers, who have not allowed a deficit in any part of their game plan or application of genetics, will be represented at all levels in swimming, including the Olympics. The legendary swim coach Doc Counsilman shows this in his telling of the story of John Kinsella and Mark Spitz. While Spitz was more of a natural swimmer and, according to Counsilman, adopted a more "relaxed" attitude to training, Kinsella embraced his drive and ability to outwork Spitz and both of them ended up breaking world records.

Swimmers who struggle to identify themselves readily in either of these categories may wish to consider if their application in the pool is sufficient or if they are failing to prepare effectively in areas such as diet, injury and illness prevention.

Question – choose which statement of the two given across the line that most represents you *as a swimmer.*

	A	B
1	I just turn up – my natural ability prevails	I generally do well when I work at it
2	I've been referred to as 'talented' or 'gifted' as a swimmer	I've been referred to as a 'grafter'
3	I've not really thought about how I apply myself – I just get on with it	I have to apply myself all of the time to get good results
4	I take it as it comes, one session at a time	I have a well thought out approach to maximise my performance

Answer interpretation -
- If you have chosen all statements in the 'A' column then you are a 'natural' swimmer.
- If you have chosen all statements in the 'B' column then you are a 'masterful' swimmer.
- If you have chosen more 'A's than 'B's then you are slightly more 'natural' than 'masterful'.
- If you have chosen more 'B's than 'A's then you are slightly more 'masterful' than 'natural'.

Natural

Overview
- Your responses suggest you apply your genetic gifts in a natural way.
- Development and progression for you will be easier than most and you will have the potential to achieve at high levels compared to most of your peers.

Key strengths
- It is easy for you to apply your genetic gifts.
- Agility and co-ordination will come easier to you than most.

Possible weaknesses & possible blind spots
- Because of the ease of past success, you are more likely to fail to plan effectively or put in the required base work to maintain your previous achievements. This may lead to inconsistency in performance and some frustration on your part.
- You are more likely to rock up to a competition and go and do your thing. You would benefit from a more robust approach to planning your races and thinking through where you can make the difference.
- You should keep in mind the old adage that 'when talent doesn't work, work beats talent'.
- Because your natural talents have generally tended to give you the results you desired, you will not be making the most of all attributes to improve your performance (these will include things like diet, injury and illness prevention, recovery programmes and taking appropriate rest).

Value to and impact on the squad
- Your natural abilities are admired by squad members and when you apply this, you are a beacon for achievement.
- Because it appears to come too easy for you, you may sometimes find other squad members are envious or even frustrated with you.

Creating your ideal environment – training and competition
- Your preference would be for the environment to be relaxed so you can go about applying your given talents.

Masterful

Overview
- Your responses suggest you apply your genetic gifts in a masterful way.
- You benefit from ensuring that your game plan for training and competition is well rounded.
- Applying yourself well will mean that you have the potential to achieve success.

Key strengths
- You are more able than most to apply your genetic gifts in a well thought through way.
- You are likely to pay more attention to the complete approach (diet, rest, recovery, strength, speed, power and finesse) and this is an advantage.
- You are more likely to plan and strategise for development and events and this will give you an edge over rivals who do not.

Possible weaknesses & possible blind spots
- As it can be necessary for you to work for your success, you should plan meticulously on every aspect of swimming.
- Your diet should be excellent, recovery and rest programmes thought through and you attention to finesse, speed, strength and power all in place and appropriately balanced.
- You probably get frustrated at some swimmers for who success appears to come naturally to. You should keep in mind the old adage that 'when talent doesn't work, work beats talent'.

Value to and impact on the squad
- You will often be viewed as the grafter of the team. This, coupled with your well thought through approach means you are viewed by others as solid and the complete package.
- Your work ethic will be admired by the squad and the coaching team.

Creating your ideal environment – training and competition
- You prefer the environment where you are able to work on all aspects of your game plan in a considered and constructive way.

4. Physical Application

This section of the system looks at how the body responds to conditions of training and competition. All swimmers will respond in a different way and at different rates and this gives you clues as to how you should approach training and competition – both in and out of the pool. The system splits swimmers into three categories being fast, medium and slow responders.

Fast responders produce good results from relatively short periods of focussed training. They like to go fast and will sometimes have trouble in holding back. Whilst this is good news in terms of preparation for events; it does come with problems such as high muscle damage, a lack of consistency and some frustration with that based on the previous ease at which they got results. Fast responders generally form less than 20% of the population.

Medium responders make up the majority of the population and will need solid training programmes to produce good results. They will need to prepare and pay attention to injury and illness prevention. They are more likely to compete effectively over a wider range of events and distances.

Slow responders get results from putting work in. High achievers from this category will develop pride in doing the work and doing it consistently. They have the ability to recover quicker and would often have less muscle damage. It will often be true that slow responders will have lots of energy.

Again, it is important to state that swimmers from each of the fast, medium and slow responder categories are able to compete successfully at any level.

Question – choose which statement of the three given across the line that most represents you *as a swimmer.*

	A	B	C
1	I get good results from short periods of focussed training	I need a good run of training sessions to produce results	I need to graft hard to produce results
2	I have trouble holding back in training	I produce balanced performances in training	I work hard in training to produce results
3	My recovery is relatively slow after training or events – my muscles are often sore for the next session	My recovery is okay – I'm generally good to go for the next session	My recovery is fast – I can't wait to do it all again
4	I don't have to plan and strategise to get good results – I just turn up and do my thing	I have to think through what I'm doing to get the best results	I have to plan carefully in advance to get the best results

Answer interpretation -
- If you have mainly chosen statements in the 'A' column then you are likely to be a fast responder.
- If you have mainly chosen statements in the 'B' column then you are likely to be a medium responder.
- If you have mainly chosen statements in the 'C' column then you are likely to be a slow responder.

Fast Responder

Overview
- You are a fast responder and only a minority of the population has this trait.
- You like to go fast and have the ability to achieve good results quickly.

Key strengths
- You get fit quickly, sharpen for competition faster than your peers and get good results quickly.
- You have a tendency to be strong and able to build muscle quickly.
- You have the ability to succeed.

Possible weaknesses & possible blind spots
- You may overlook putting in the base work to maintain your stamina as, in the past, you have been able to sharpen up quickly and get good results. This may lead to inconsistency in performance and frustration.
- You have more of a tendency to put weight on (be this general weight or muscle) so you need to keep this under review.
- You will need to monitor muscle damage and pay particular attention to recovery, making sure you have appropriate rest between training sessions.

Value to and impact on the squad
- You will be admired for your ability to respond positively to intensive work and your ability to sharpen well for competitions. This will be a frustration to other squad members though who have to work hard and over sustained periods to achieve what you can in such a short space of time.

Suggestions for development
- You will need to understand and employ methods to avoid muscle damage and to ensure your recovery is adequate for the next training session.
- You should understand the impact of food choices and whether this results in any excess weight gain (general or muscular).
- You will need to understand the importance of, and embrace longer stamina sets as this will enhance your performance.
- You will benefit from a consistent approach to progressive training cycles.

Creating your ideal environment – training and competition
- You respond well to, and enjoy short bursts of intensive work - particularly where you can go fast.
- You will benefit though from balanced speed and endurance work.
- The training environment should be relaxed.
- You will require a detailed sharpening plan for target competitions and you will need to stick to this.
- You will benefit from frequent racing.

Motivating and engaging
- You will be motivated by shorter sets and races where you can go fast.
- You will be engaged where you can see the benefits and outcomes of more endurance and stamina building work.
- You will be motivated when proactive feedback is given on the effort you put in.

Medium Responder

Overview
- You are a medium responder and if you apply yourself to training and preparation you will be successful over a range of events and distances.

Key strengths
- You are able to produce balanced performances over a range of events if you train effectively.
- You respond well to balanced training.
- You have the ability to succeed if you apply yourself.

Possible weaknesses & possible blind spots
- You may become frustrated at the length of time and the effort it takes to succeed, especially when compared to fast responders.
- You may not concentrate sufficiently on, or pay enough attention to the speed work which is necessary to sharpen you up for competitions.
- You may not recognise the positive impact your application and dedication has on the squad.

Value to and impact on the squad
- You can demonstrate that you can apply yourself consistently to get results and this will be a positive influence on other squad members – particularly the more junior ones.

Suggestions for development
- You tend to recover well and are usually ready for the next training session or race. You do however need to be mindful of, and prepare for illness and injury prevention as you apply yourself hard in the pool. You will therefore need to eat nutritious and healthy food, warm up properly and take the appropriate rest between training sessions.

- You will benefit from carefully planned training cycles which will bring you to your best at target meets.
- You will need to incorporate and apply yourself to speed work in your training regimes.

Creating your ideal environment – training and competition
- As a medium responder you will benefit from longer training builds and key sets which are repeated throughout the cycle in which to compare your performance.
- You will like a range of activity in the pool in which to apply yourself as you can clearly see the benefits of a balanced approach.

Motivating and engaging
- You will be motivated when proactive feedback is given on the effort you put in.
- You will be motivated when you have a range of events in which to compete.

Slow Responder

Overview
- You are a slow responder and you can achieve success by putting the work in.
- If you develop pride in applying yourself to work and doing this consistently, you will do well over the long term – particularly as you have high energy levels and recover quicker.

Key strengths
- You will have the ability to succeed if you put the hard work in.
- You are likely to develop a habit of taking pride in things like mileage and consistency and from this you will get your results.
- You are likely to produce lower levels of lactate than your peers which will help you train harder and for longer periods and compete over a wider range of distances.
- You have high energy levels as well as the ability to recover quickly.

Possible weaknesses & possible blind spots
- You may become frustrated at the length of time and the effort it takes to succeed, especially when compared to fast responders.
- You may not concentrate sufficiently on or pay enough attention to the speed work which is necessary to sharpen you up for competitions.
- You may not recognise the positive impact your application and dedication has on the squad.

Value to and impact on the squad
- You can demonstrate that you can apply yourself consistently to get results and your brilliant work ethic will be a positive influence on other squad members – particularly the more junior ones.

Suggestions for development
- You tend to recover well and are usually ready for the next training session or race.
- You are usually keen to get back in the pool as you have high energy levels and a great work ethic.
- You do however need to be mindful of, and prepare for illness and injury prevention as you apply yourself hard in the pool. You will therefore need to eat nutritious and healthy food, warm up properly and take the appropriate rest between training sessions.
- You will benefit from carefully planned training cycles which will bring you to your best at target meets.
- You may need to have fewer target meets in the year at which to perform your PBs as you will generally be in longer training cycles than fast or medium responders.
- You will need to incorporate and apply yourself to speed work in your training regimes.
- You should ensure that you develop good quality muscles through a range of activities.
- You should take more comfort in the fact that the way you apply yourself has a positive impact on the squad.

Creating your ideal environment – training and competition
- You will benefit from longer training builds than most, with key sets which are repeated throughout the cycle in which to compare your progress.
- You will like a range of activity in the pool in which to apply yourself as you can clearly see the benefits of a balanced approach.
- You will benefit from a high training load with high intensity both for your development as well as your satisfaction in shining above other squad members. Whilst shorter, pacier style sets may not be that easy for you to 'swim into', they are an important part of your preparation.

Motivating and engaging

- You will be motivated by goals set against high intensity and high yardage – excelling where others can't keep up.
- You will be motivated when proactive feedback is given on the effort you put in.
- You will be motivated by longer term goals to work towards.
- You will be motivated when you have a range of events over a range of distances in which to compete.

5. Physiological Application

This category is concerned with how the body carries out physical functions. Systems in the body play major roles in the reception and transmission of signals that provide your functionality. This is not a preference expressed by the mind; it's the way you are made. It does manifest itself in how you do like to function - because you are more adept at doing it.

The Lewis Parnell system uses the categories of finesse, speed, strength and power. Finesse is on one end of the spectrum with power being on the other in the order shown:

- A 'finesse' swimmer is described as one who likes complexity of co-ordination, endurance and rhythm.
- A 'speed' swimmer likes agility, reaction speeds and velocity.
- A 'strength' swimmer likes the intensity, the build to maximum and likes stamina pursuits.
- A 'power' swimmer likes fast tempos, explosiveness and acceleration.

Question – choose which word of the four given across the line that most represents you *as a swimmer.*

	A	B	C	D
1	Co-ordinated	Agile	Intense	Explosive
2	Endurance	Reacts well	Stamina	Acceleration
3	Rhythmic	Fast paced	Build to max	Fast Tempo

Answer interpretation -
- If you have mainly chosen words in the 'A' column then you are likely to be a finesse swimmer.
- If you have mainly chosen words in the 'B' column then you are likely to be a speed swimmer.
- If you have mainly chosen words in the 'C' column then you are likely to be a strength swimmer.

- If you have mainly chosen words in the 'D' column then you are likely to be a power swimmer.

It will also generally be true that:
- Finesse swimmers would like longer distance events and training sets in which to deploy their rhythm and 'swim into'.
- Speed swimmers would like medium to short events and broken training sets with short rest so that they can swim fast all the way through.
- Strength swimmers would like medium to short events and build training sets with medium rest so they can 'max-out' at the end.
- Power swimmers would like shorter events and short training sets with ample rest so they can go bananas.

Finesse Swimmer

Overview
- You are a finesse swimmer and like the complexity of coordination, endurance and rhythm.
- Your ability to maintain control and posture in the water is envied by others and once you have found your 'sweet spot' you will be hard to beat.

Key strengths
- You adore the complexity of co-ordination and this is a strength when it comes to technique and balance within swimming.
- You like rhythmic endurance so will naturally be able to settle into sets and complete work in the pool to a high standard. Co-ordination and rhythm is a deadly combination when applied in race conditions.
- The ease of your technique saves you energy and when you find your 'sweet spot' you are able to swim past other types of swimmers, particularly in longer events.

- You are able to understand the finer aspects of stroke technique and the agility required.
- You are more likely than others to develop a race strategy and this will help you out perform rivals.

Possible weaknesses & possible blind spots
- You may find it hard to build muscle quickly. For you, strength and power doesn't come quickly and needs work. These are areas for improvement and you may tend to ignore them as you get slow returns for your work.
- Shorter events may not be so much fun for you as rapid turnover of arms and thrashing about with the legs leads to a loss of co-ordination and agility.
- You are unlikely to be explosive or able to react and accelerate as quickly as others. This deficit requires planning to mitigate the risks to you during competition.

Value to and impact on the squad
- Your good technique will be a good example to the rest of the squad and younger squad members.
- You've probably already been complemented, pointed out or been demonstrating to the rest of the squad!

Suggestions for development
- You will need to find ways to build (the right sort of) muscle whether this is through gym work, light weights or general fitness activities.
- Strength and power doesn't come quickly and requires work, so when you come across these types of set in training, embrace them.
- You are unlikely to be explosive or able to react and accelerate as quickly as others. This deficit requires planning to mitigate the risks to you during competition.

Creating your ideal environment – training and competition
- You will like opportunities to complete longer sets and longer distances where you can develop rhythm and swim into your 'sweet spot'.

Motivating and engaging
- You will be motivated and engaged by longer sets and swims where you can develop rhythm and swim into your 'sweet spot'.

Speed Swimmer

Overview
- You are a speed swimmer and have good agility.
- You will be able to react fast in the pool and swim at high velocities.

Key strengths
- You have agility and the ability to swim fast. This is a deadly combination at any time but very effective when deployed in races.
- You have better than normal reactions and this is a great ability to have when in race conditions.
- You are efficient in most things that you do.

Possible weaknesses & possible blind spots
- You may find it hard to build muscle quickly. For you, strength and power doesn't come quickly as others and needs work. These are areas for improvement and you may tend to ignore them as you get slow returns for your work.
- Your reaction and agility partly offsets any deficiency in explosiveness and acceleration but these would be areas to work on when training and be mindful of in competition so you can mitigate risks from fast finishing swimmers.

Value to and impact on the squad
- Your reaction speed, velocity and agility are the things you will be admired for.
- People like to share a lane with you because you are fast and as you are agile, you're unlikely to bump into them!

Suggestions for development
- You will need to find ways to build (the right sort of) muscle whether this is through gym work, light weights or general fitness activities.
- Your reaction and agility partly offsets any deficiency in explosiveness and acceleration but these would be areas to work on when training and be mindful of in competition so you can mitigate risks from fast finishing swimmers.

Creating your ideal environment – training and competition
- You will like opportunities to swim fast and employ your agility and reaction speeds off the starts and the turns.

Motivating and engaging
- You like to swim fast, perhaps over shorter sets and will be motivated and engaged where you can revel in your agility and reaction speeds off the starts and the turns.

Strength Swimmer

Overview
- You are a strength swimmer and like the intensity of it all.
- Your levels of stamina will be the envy of other swimmers as too will your ability to excel at building to maximum performances.

Key strengths
- You have the ability to build muscle and to blast your way through training sets and competition events.
- You have agility too and this, coupled with your ability to change speed, is a deadly combination when deployed in competition.

Possible weaknesses & possible blind spots
- You will have some holes in your technique which will be hidden by your strength. These may be small but, if corrected, will help you swim faster.
- You may rely on your strength and stamina to pull you through. This could mean you leave it too late in a race.
- Your strength and stamina partly offsets any deficiency in explosiveness and your ability to accelerate but these would be areas to work on when training and be mindful of in competition so you can mitigate risks from fast finishing swimmers.

Value to and impact on the squad
- You will be admired for your strength and ability to build in sets to a magnificent crescendo.
- Your good levels of stamina will set the standard for others to achieve and will be infectious during longer and more difficult sets.

Suggestions for development
- You will have some holes in your technique which will be hidden by your strength. These may be small but, if corrected, will help you swim faster.
- You may rely on your strength and stamina to pull you through. This could mean you leave it too late in a race.
- Apply yourself in speed sets.
- Your strength and stamina partly offset any deficiency in explosiveness and your ability to accelerate but these would be areas to work on when training and be

mindful of in competition so you can mitigate risks from fast finishing swimmers.

Creating your ideal environment – training and competition
- You will like opportunities for intensive training which build up to your maximum.

Motivating and engaging
- You will like the intensity of training over medium sets and will be motivated and engaged when you are given the chance to the build up to your maximum.

Power Swimmer

Overview
- You are a power swimmer and enjoy fast tempos, explosiveness and acceleration.
- Your opposition might not see your change of pace until it's too late.

Key strengths
- You are explosive and can accelerate faster than most of your peers which is a deadly combination when deployed in competition.
- You have the ability to build muscle and to blast your way through training sets and competition events.

Possible weaknesses & possible blind spots
- You will have some holes in your technique which will be hidden by your power. These may be small but, if corrected, will help you swim faster.
- You may rely on your power to pull you through. This could mean you leave it too late in a race.
- Your power partly offsets any deficiency in stamina and efficient technique but these would be areas to work on when training and be mindful of in competition so you don't run out of steam before the finish.

Value to and impact on the squad
- You will be admired for your all-out speed and the ability to swim fast at a high tempo.
- When the fast work starts, you'll probably entertain squad members with the tidal waves you create from your power!

Suggestions for development
- You will have some holes in your technique which will be hidden by your power. These may be small but, if corrected, will help you swim faster.
- You may rely on your power to pull you through. This could mean you leave it too late in a race. Work hard on speed sets in training.
- Your power partly offsets any deficiency in stamina and efficient technique but these would be areas to work on when training and be mindful of in competition so you don't run out of steam before the finish.

Creating your ideal environment – training and competition
- You will like short sharp sets where the tempo is fast and you can demonstrate your explosiveness and acceleration.

Motivating and engaging
- You will be motivated and engaged when the distances are short and the tempo is fast and when you can demonstrate your explosiveness and acceleration.

6. Psychosocial Application

Psychosocial Application relates to development and interaction with the social environment. As you interact, you have your conscious state and your less conscious state of mind. Analysis in this section points toward solutions for individual challenges in interacting with the social environment. You may be introvert or extrovert, prefer spur of the moment situations or controlled ones, you may have high will power or may need assurance, be able to focus or be easily distracted.

There is no best way of interacting; but understanding how you do will help you achieve. The system uses the categories of 'direct action' swimmer, 'conscientious dependable' swimmer, 'happy radiant' swimmer and 'clear analytical' swimmer.

- Direct action swimmers are generally extrovert with high levels of energy. They are direct and always on the go.
- Conscientious dependable swimmers are inclusive and democratic. They focus on values and are personal in style as well as showing their desire for understanding.
- Happy radiant swimmers are strongly extroverted, positive and friendly. They are interested in social interaction, often persuasive and inclusive.
- Clear analytical swimmers are introverted and want to know more about what's going on around them. They like precision and need time to complete their desired analysis.

Question – This question relates to you as a person - choose which word of the four given across the line that most represents you *as a person*:

	A	B	C	D
1	Action oriented	Realist	Sociable	Analytical
2	Able	Controlled	Positive	Inquisitive
3	Direct	Dependable	Persuasive	Honourable
4	Extrovert	Democratic	Inclusive	Thinker
5	Highly energised	Grounded	Creative	Precise

Answer interpretation -

- If you have mainly chosen words in the 'A' column then you are likely to be a direct action swimmer.
- If you have mainly chosen words in the 'B' column then you are likely to be a conscientious dependable swimmer.
- If you have mainly chosen words in the 'C' column then you are likely to be a happy radiant swimmer.
- If you have mainly chosen words in the 'D' column then you are likely to be a clear analytical swimmer.

It will also generally be true that:

- Direct Action swimmers will want to have challenging training and can't wait for the main set – bring it on!
- Conscientious Dependable swimmers will want the training to be ordered but there still to be some social time with squad members and they will want Coach to explain why they are doing things in a certain way.
- Happy Radiant swimmers will want the session to be varied and interesting where things are fun, lively and above all challenging.
- Clear Analytical swimmers will want training which is ordered and the rules applied along with time to consider what Coach has told them.

Direct Action Swimmer

Overview
- You are an extrovert with high levels of energy.
- You are direct and always on the go.
- Your energy and action means that you are a beacon for the squad.
- You'll probably be the one running the company at the end of the day.

Key strengths
- Your psychosocial strengths are abundant.
- You are enthusiastic and optimistic.
- The combination of being intuitive, focussed and driven will serve you well.
- You are extroverted and seen by many as being brave, daring and bold.
- Your attributes will help you focus on your longer term goals and keep you motivated in the pursuit of your desired achievements.

Possible weaknesses & possible blind spots
- You may not be so aware of the 'here and now' as you have your plan and driving yourself towards it.
- You sometimes do not actively listen to what's being said to you so will miss key information and advice which could be utilised.
- You may come across as already knowing the answer or subject matter being relayed to you and this might frustrate the donor.
- You may spend unnecessary energy on battling for power and control.

Value to and impact on the squad
- You are an enthusiastic motivator and your determination will be an excellent example to other squad members.
- You will be seen by others as bold, daring and brave – one of the leaders.
- Some will however perceive you as arrogant, aggressive or likely to rock the boat for the sake of it. Some may even find your urgency and drive causes them stress.

Communications
- Communications should be direct, well structured and to the point.
- Information should be quickly and clearly delivered but in sufficient detail not to allow you to come to wrong conclusions.
- You like facts so these should be included and you'll turn off when someone delivers the messages slowly or rambles.

Suggestions for development
- You should take the opportunity to slow down and think things through properly – it's often difficult for you as you drive forward at such a fast pace.
- You should also take the opportunity to analyse your own thoughts and feelings to make sure they are rational and balanced.
- You should make time to relax and develop relaxation techniques which work for you.
- You should concentrate on the 'here and now' when in training and make sure you are actively listening.
- Try to keep your energies concentrated on the things that will matter to your performance and not waste them unnecessarily on battling for control and power.

Creating your ideal environment – training and competition
- You generally tend to dislike or avoid routine tasks so training needs to be varied and challenging. It does however need to be ordered and thought through.
- Both training and competition will be results oriented. Expected results should be set by the coaching team but you will have already thought them through and come to your own conclusions.
- You are most comfortable during competition when you have thought through the process and ordered it - you are clear what you need to do, the order of events and what will be happening both inside and outside the sports centre.
- You would prefer an environment where there isn't too much social chit-chat or long periods of inactivity where social frivolity could become a frustration.
- You like environments where there is stimulation and worthy competitors.
- You would benefit from an environment where you take time to have personal space and force yourself to relax.

Motivating and engaging
- You will be motivated by challenge and stretching targets.
- You will be motivated by competition with others and particularly against worthy competitors.
- You need to be given the target and then left alone to get on with achieving it - but you need to know you can call on people when you need to.
- You require recognition of your achievements.

Conscientious Dependable Swimmer

Overview
- You are inclusive and democratic and therefore a valued member of the team.
- You focus on values and are personal in style.
- In developing your swimming, you will benefit from your desire for understanding.

Key strengths
- Your psychosocial strengths are strong.
- You are a finisher and this will provide you with advantages over your peers.
- Your desire to understand as well as your awareness of the technical aspects will benefit you in receiving information and utilising it.
- You will be able to use your good judgment on relationships to form deep relationships with other squad members which will be of benefit in the often chaotic world of swimming.

Possible weaknesses & possible blind spots
- You tend to get stressed if information is delivered too quickly or you are not given time to assimilate it. That's just the way you are but it is difficult for you where there is a fast tempo in training.
- You may give up easily if you feel isolated.
- You lose focus when lacking intellectual challenge.

Value to and impact on the squad
- Your inclusivity and approach to democracy means you are a valuable member of the squad and valued by others.
- You value individuals and develop good strong relationships with them – this builds a good solid foundation and will increase the resistance and durability of the whole team.

- You are admired by and inspire others because of your sincerity, loyalty and ability to finish things.
- Some will however think you aren't particularly interested in them, especially if they are overly social and direct.

Communications
- Communications should be clear and logical.
- They should be delivered with supporting facts and devoid of too much dressing, flowering and unnecessary detail.
- You will deliver on communications so don't necessarily need messages to be checked too many times.

Suggestions for development
- You should develop coping strategies for dealing with stressful situations or people (usually direct action swimmers) who cause you stress.
- You may benefit from being more open about your feelings.
- You could consider working on building relationships, however uncomfortable this can be with people you do not naturally find common ground with.
- You should definitely consider and set yourself stretching actions.
- Try and have an up-front discussion with the coaching team about the session so you will have time to take in the information and ask questions.

Creating your ideal environment – training and competition
- You like an environment which allows you to prepare adequately for the session activities or the competition ahead.
- You would prefer an environment where there isn't too much social chit-chat or long periods of inactivity where social frivolity could become a frustration.

- You thrive in an environment where you are included and can contribute but are not forced into the spotlight.
- You like it when things are clearly stated, there is order to things and there are no surprise changes. This enables you get down to the hard work of completing and finishing things in your usual way.
- You prefer activities in which your mind is absorbed.
- You do not like to be bossed or pressured, but you do like to be given the respect for how good you are at applying yourself.
- You like environments where support or reassurance is there, should you require them.

Motivating and engaging
- You are motivated by an environment where you are included but not thrust into the limelight.
- You require recognition for your achievements and your dependable and solid approach.
- You require the information and are motivated by the opportunity to apply it, on your own.
- You are engaged by people seeking your opinion.

Happy Radiant Swimmer

Overview
- You are lively and strongly extroverted.
- Your positivity and friendliness is liked by practically everyone and you are a great person to have on the squad.
- You are interested in social interaction, often persuasive and inclusive.
- You will be open to new ideas, training and competition strategies and prepared to give things a go which will be to your advantage.

Key strengths
- Your psychosocial strengths are abundant.
- You are good fun to be around. Being social, extrovert, lively and friendly means you settle well and often find your training and competition environments comfortable.
- Your 'cup is always half full' mindset will help you overcome obstacles, setbacks and hard training cycles.
- You are able to see the bigger picture and the longer term goals which helps in getting through the hard work of here and now.
- Your creativity and spontaneity allows you to adapt easily to change and take advantage of any opportunities presented by new or different training techniques.

Possible weaknesses & possible blind spots
- You can easily be distracted by others or other things going on around you.
- You also have a tendency to amuse yourself in a non-productive way. These things can lead you to failing to apply yourself in the best way that you are capable of - and you may even lose your place in sets!
- You are likely to take advice and information at face value and accept it, even though probing further and understanding more would be of benefit to you.
- You will tend to take criticism or justified feedback as personal criticism, possibly smarting over it for days.
- Your lively persona will sometimes appear as disruptive or even overpowering to some.
- You will have a tendency to put other's first, worry unnecessarily and overlook your own needs, often to help or please others.

Value to and impact on the squad

- You are a great person to have on the squad.
- You are social, participative and involved.
- You inspire with motivation, energy and direction.
- Not only are you infectious with your friendliness and enthusiasm, you are inclusive, democratic and an advocate - and others like you for that.
- You will tend to be the one organising the social calendar – you just can't help it!
- You may not naturally respond to people who aren't like you – you will tend to overlook them or may even have a short fuse with them.

Communications

- Communications should be delivered in a positive, open and enthusiastic way.
- You are happy with a more casual and informal style.
- You respond better when references are made to your past successes and when you receive praise.
- You will benefit from lots of short contact or touching base between sets and reps.
- You will need to know what the expected outcomes are.

Suggestions for development

- You should ensure that you plan ahead effectively as often your self-selected activities keep you very busy and away from the important tasks which need to be considered.
- You should concentrate on the task in hand and try to finish it appropriately, not becoming distracted.
- You should not reject negative feedback out of hand as it may give you valuable insights and you should try not to take criticism personally.
- You may benefit from aspiring to perfection in fewer things than trying to achieve a good level in all things.

- You should ask for the reasoning behind the instructions given by the coaching team - so that you don't just take them at face value; you understand what's trying to be achieved.
- You should try and put yourself first on more occasions and worry less about looking after and trying to please others.

Creating your ideal environment – training and competition
- You like training and competition environments where you are allowed to express your emotions – how you feel is important to you.
- You like lots of opportunities for interaction and social contact and being with like minded people.
- You like environments that have variety and where flexibility and change happen.
- You would benefit from an environment which has structure to contain your disposition to become distracted but allows you time and space to be creative.
- You like opportunities where you can constantly develop and extend your skills.

Motivating and engaging
- You are motivated by being noticed and congratulated for your efforts and achievements. Where things go well, they should be recalled, recognised and praised - publically if possible.
- You will be motivated by lively people of a similar type to you.
- You will respond to reward for performance, the better and more diverse the reward is, the higher the motivation – even if it is praise alone.
- You will be motivated by a nurturing environment and one where you are able to be creative.
- Colour, image and sound will be your motivating mediums.

Clear Analytical Swimmer

Overview

- You want to know more about what's going on around you and understand it – this will be an advantage to you.
- You generally like to keep yourself to yourself, like precision and need time to complete your desired analysis.
- You will bring a unique perspective to the squad which will be valued as it is grounded in reality.

Key strengths

- Your psychosocial strengths are solid.
- You are logical, seek perfection and can see the way to achieving your goals and this provides you with advantages over your peers.
- Your desire to understand as well as your awareness of the technical aspects and attention to detail will benefit you in receiving information and utilising it.
- You will be able to use your good judgment, honesty and sincerity to form good relationships with other squad members which will be of benefit in the often chaotic world of swimming.
- You will always be thinking, which is a valuable asset to have when looking to develop your swimming or an advantage over others.

Possible weaknesses & possible blind spots

- Your desire for clarity and precision may lead you to disengage or not perform to your best if information delivered does not meet your high expectations.
- Your cautious approach and tendency to keep yourself to yourself may mean you are overlooked.
- You tend to lack confidence and underestimate your contribution.

- You may hide your feelings until it is too late.
- You lose focus when lacking intellectual challenge.
- You can over analyse things or miss out on good advice if it is not delivered with a suitable logical reason.
- You may appear critical – especially when under pressure.
- You tend to bring your life problems into the pool with you and let it affect you.
- You may tend to agree too easily in order to avoid confrontation.

Value to and impact on the squad
- You bring a unique contribution to the squad in terms of realism, well thought through concepts which are based on logical and detailed analysis.
- You have a better understanding than most on how it all fits together, where the coaches are bringing you to and how technique works - and you are able to relay this if required or asked.
- You will tend to hold back in getting involved or giving advice when the reality is you have something valuable to give.
- You encourage a calm environment which is welcomed by other squad members when they are applying themselves in training or preparing for competitions.
- You develop strong relationships with some squad members which creates a solid foundation and will increase the resistance and durability of the whole team.
- You may however be seen by some as being distant or uninterested in them or the squad.

Communications
- Communications should be delivered sincerely and in a more serious than casual manner.
- There should be no confrontation and you would benefit in receiving the message if you are at ease.
- You will need the detail, particularly if there are any changes being made.
- You will need time to consider and ask questions.
- You need people to clearly state what they mean.

Suggestions for development
- You should try and see the benefit of new and alternative ways of doing things and try to embrace these more readily.
- You could consider being more open with others; particularly trusted squad members and the coaching team.
- You should force yourself to make decisions on things, coming to definite conclusions and then following these through.
- You could develop coping strategies for dealing with stressful situations or people (usually direct action swimmers) who cause you stress.
- Try and have an up-front discussion with the coaching team about the session so you will have time to take in the information and ask questions.
- Try to take something out of the set, even when you can't see the point of it, it doesn't challenge you or other squad members are being disruptive.

Creating your ideal environment – training and competition
- You like a safe, calm and ordered environment where people observe the rules and give you the space and time to do your thing.
- You like harmonious, non-pressured environments where you have the time to consider.

- You thrive in an environment where you are included and can contribute but are not forced into the spotlight.
- In competition environments you like to have free time which isn't taken up by too much social chit-chat or long periods of inactivity where social frivolity could become a frustration.
- You like to have the whole picture and the detail so you can think it through and time to discuss it, if you so wish.
- You prefer training activities in which your mind is absorbed.
- You like environments where support or reassurance is there, should you require it.
- In training you would prefer tried and tested sets and schedules and would benefit from low-key ways of being set challenges and low key ways to receive feedback – especially if it is positive.

Motivating and engaging
- You are motivated by the detail, being in possession of the facts and the bigger picture and by being given longer term security.
- You are engaged through being asked how you feel, when your opinion is sought and respect given for the considered way you apply your attributes.
- You will be engaged when you feel the environment is safe and where there is sufficient activity for you to learn, improve and grow.
- You will be motivated by achieving your own goals rather than competing with others.

Contact details: Lewis Parnell Ltd
www.lewisparnell.com
lewisparnell@btinternet.com
Twitter: @lewisparnellST

*Lewis Parnell are happy to complete a profile for you –
visit www.lewisparnell.com*

*We can complete whole squad profiles to assist coaches
understand what types of swimmers they are coaching,
how to best communicate with them and how to get the
best performance.*

*Lewis Parnell are committed to raising the standard of
swimming across the world – look out for our swimming
technique system and resources.*

www.ingramcontent.com/pod-product-compliance
Lightning Source LLC
Chambersburg PA
CBHW071744020426
42331CB00008B/2164